Jimmy Luther

I Talk You Talk Press

CONTENTS

I Talk You Talk Press

1. JIMMY LUTHER GETS A JOB

Jimmy Luther is in math class. He is sitting at the back of the classroom. It's almost lunchtime. It is sunny and warm. Jimmy feels sleepy. He doesn't like math, so he's not listening to the teacher.

The classroom door opens. Mrs Catwell comes into the classroom. The math teacher goes to talk to her. Then he looks at the students.

"Jimmy Luther. Mrs Catwell wants to talk to you. Our lesson is almost finished. You can go now."

Jimmy stands up and leaves the classroom. Mrs Catwell and Jimmy walk to her office.

"Come in and sit down, Jimmy," she says.

Mrs Catwell is the school's careers advisor. She gives students advice about jobs. It is Jimmy's first time to go to her office. He looks around the room. There are many pamphlets. Jimmy sees pamphlets about many kinds of jobs. There are also pamphlets about universities.

Why does she want to talk to me? he thinks.

Mrs Catwell sits behind her desk. Jimmy sits in a chair. He looks at Mrs Catwell.

Jimmy's school has a special programme. Students go to work outside school for a week. It's called the work experience programme. Students experience working life. They try different jobs and think about their future jobs.

"Next week is 'work experience week' for your class," says Mrs Catwell. "All students will work somewhere. I have found a job for everyone in your class. But I haven't found a job for you. I need information from you, but you didn't fill in any of the forms."

"What forms?" asks Jimmy.

"The form about your hobbies. The form about your plans for the future and the job application form."

"Oh! Those forms! I forgot," says Jimmy.

"Well it is now very late. Maybe I can't find a job for you."

"That's OK, Mrs Catwell," says Jimmy. "Don't worry about it."

Jimmy thinks this is good. Everyone in my class will go to work for a week. There will be no classes. I'll have a week's vacation.

"Next week, you have to come to school. I talked to Mrs Wilson in the library. You can clean all the storerooms in the library."

Jimmy is not happy.

Mrs Catwell looks at him. "You don't want to help Mrs Wilson. I know. A job outside the school is better for you."

Mrs Catwell likes Jimmy. He is a very lazy boy, but he is always happy.

"Come on, Jimmy! Help me to find you a job! What are you interested in?"

Jimmy looks at the floor. He looks up. He looks at the wall behind Mrs Catwell's head. There is a picture of a basket of vegetables. Jimmy is very, very hungry.

"Food," he says. "Food."

He is thinking about his lunch. He stops listening to Mrs Catwell.

"Very good Jimmy! That's great! A restaurant. I can find a restaurant for you. You can work in a restaurant kitchen for a week."

The bell rings. It's lunchtime. Jimmy stands up.

"Yes, Jimmy. You can go now. I will give you information about your job tomorrow," says Mrs Catwell

"Thanks," says Jimmy.

What job is she talking about? I'm not going to think about it. It's lunchtime, thinks Jimmy.

2. JIMMY LUTHER AT WORK

"Jimmy! Jimmy!" shouts Mrs Catwell. "I found a job for you."

Jimmy stops walking. He is going to PE class. He doesn't mind if he is late.

"It's good news, Jimmy. You can work at a restaurant in the centre of Melbourne for a week. Are you happy?"

"I think so," says Jimmy.

Mrs Catwell gives Jimmy the piece of paper. "You start on Monday. It's a vegetarian restaurant. They are only open at lunchtimes. You start work at 6:00am. You finish at 2:30pm. They will give you breakfast and lunch. That's good."

Is it good? thinks Jimmy. He doesn't know.

"Uh, thank you Mrs Catwell," he says.

Next Monday, Jimmy gets up at 5:00am. His mother came home from work at 3:00am. She is sleeping. His little sister is sleeping too. Jimmy puts milk and cornflakes on the table for his sister. He makes some peanut butter sandwiches and puts them in her lunch box. Usually Jimmy goes to school after his sister. He helps her in the mornings. Today he can't help her.

He rides his bike. It takes 40 minutes to get to the centre of the city. There are trains and buses from Jimmy's area to the city, but he has no money. He doesn't want to ask his mother for money. She works very hard as a night cleaner. She only has a little money for the family.

The restaurant is called Natural. Jimmy finds the back door of the restaurant. There are other bicycles behind the restaurant. He opens the back door, and goes inside. The restaurant kitchen is very busy. A woman is washing vegetables. Another woman is chopping vegetables.

"Are you the work experience boy?" asks the woman who is washing vegetables.

"Yes, I'm Jimmy Luther."

"We're busy today. So we are very pleased to have you here." The woman smiles. "I'm Alison."

The woman chopping vegetables smiles too. "I'm Barbara." She goes to a locker and takes out a white coat and a cap. "Put these on. Then you can wash the vegetables. When you have finished, you can chop the cabbage for me."

"OK," says Jimmy. *Washing vegetables is easy,* he thinks.

Jimmy works hard. He washes vegetables, he chops cabbage, and he washes and dries dishes. He is not very good at anything.

Jimmy drops a pot of potatoes on the floor. Alison throws them away.

He cuts his finger when he is chopping cabbage. There is a lot of blood. There is blood on the cabbage. Alison throws it away.

Jimmy breaks three glasses and a plate when he is washing dishes. He has a bad day.

It is now 2:30pm. It is the end of Jimmy's first day at work.

He takes off the coat and cap.

I'll take these home and wash them," he says. "I'll bring them back to you on Wednesday."

"What about tomorrow?" asks Alison.

"You don't want me here," says Jimmy. "I am bad at everything. You had to throw away the potatoes and the cabbage. I broke the glasses and the plate."

Alison and Barbara laugh. "Everyone makes mistakes at the start. You are learning. It's OK. You made mistakes, but you worked very hard. Come tomorrow!" says Alison.

3. JIMMY LUTHER THE VEGETABLE EATER

Jimmy is working in a restaurant. It is a vegetarian restaurant. The owners are Alison and Barbara. They cook lunch for customers every day. Jimmy's job is to wash and chop vegetables, and to do the dishes.

He starts work at 6:00am and finishes at 2:30pm. The restaurant gives him something to eat at about 8:30am and again about 11:00am.

The first day, Jimmy is very hungry. He wants to eat something nice for breakfast.

"Jimmy! Breakfast!" says Barbara. Jimmy goes to the big table in the centre of the kitchen. He looks at the bowl. "What's this?" he asks.

"It's muesli," says Barbara. "It's made from oats, nuts and fruit. It's very healthy."

Jimmy always has cornflakes for breakfast. He adds extra sugar and a lot of milk. He doesn't think the muesli will taste good, so he doesn't eat it.

By 11:00am, Jimmy is very, very hungry. Everyone in the kitchen stops work for twenty minutes to eat together.

Alison made curry for the customers. She made a lot, so the kitchen workers eat the curry too.

Jimmy thinks *I will eat it. I'm hungry.*

But when he sees it, he is not so sure. It has pumpkin and other vegetables and some white cubes. "What are the white cubes?" asks Jimmy.

"Tofu," says Alison.

Jimmy tries the curry. It doesn't taste so bad. He eats a lot.

The food in the restaurant and the food Jimmy eats at home is different. Jimmy starts to enjoy it. On Wednesday he eats the muesli for breakfast. He eats corn muffins and red beans for lunch.

On Thursday, the restaurant is not very busy. "Would you like to learn how to make a salad?" asks Barbara.

"OK," says Jimmy. Barbara shows Jimmy how to make salad dressing. She shows him how to arrange tomatoes and lettuce on plates. Jimmy thinks it looks very nice. The workers eat Jimmy's salad for lunch. Everyone says it tastes very good. Jimmy is pleased. He is not good at schoolwork, but he can make a good tomato salad!

Friday is Jimmy's last day at the restaurant. On Monday he will go back to school. He is sad. He likes Barbara and Alison. Now, he loves vegetables. He doesn't want to go back to school.

"Thank you very much," he says to Barbara and Alison. "I liked it here."

"We only open for lunch from Monday to Friday, but would you like to come back and work here in the school holidays?" asks Alison. "We will pay you, of course. We can give you a part-time job."

Jimmy is very happy, but he knows he can't do it. "I want to, but I can't," he says. "My mum works at nights, and she sleeps in the day. I have a little sister. She is only eight. In the school holidays I have to take care of her every day."

4. JIMMY LUTHER SURPRISES MR HARRISON

Jimmy Luther lives with his mother and little sister, Joanna. His mother works at nights. Jimmy often looks after his little sister. He helps his mother because she is always very tired. Jimmy makes breakfast for Joanna. He makes sandwiches for lunch. Usually Jimmy makes peanut butter or jam sandwiches.

In the evening, the family eats cheap food. They eat sausages or frozen food, or spaghetti from a can. Sometimes, when there is enough money, they go out to eat hamburgers or fried chicken.

But Jimmy wants to eat different food. He worked for a week in a vegetarian restaurant. At first, the food was strange to him. He didn't want to eat it. But after a few days, he liked it very much. Jimmy thinks he can learn to cook, but he needs to get vegetables.

Jimmy's mother goes to the supermarket every Saturday. She brings home bread, biscuits, jam, cornflakes, peanut butter, sausages, frozen food, milk and soda.

"Mum," Jimmy says to his mother. "Can you buy some tomatoes and lettuce please?"

"Why?" asks his mother. She is very surprised. "You and your sister don't eat vegetables."

"I eat vegetables now," says Jimmy. "I can make a salad."

"No, Jimmy. Tomatoes are expensive. You won't eat them, and your sister won't eat them. I can't waste money."

Jimmy gives up. His mother is always tired, and she is always thinking about money.

The next day at school, Jimmy has a science class. Jimmy doesn't like science. He always fails his tests. So Jimmy is in a class for low level students. The teacher is Mr Harrison. He is 65 years old. His hobby is gardening. He will retire soon. He is happy. He can work in his garden every day.

Mr Harrison comes into the class. He looks at the students. They are reading comics. They are looking at their mobile phones. They are talking. Jimmy Luther has put his head on his desk. Mr Harrison feels sad. He looks at his lesson plan. He plans to teach the class about atoms, ions and molecules.

It is a waste of time, he thinks. *These students are not interested. I will talk and talk. I will draw pictures on the blackboard. I will ask questions. No one will answer me. Maybe I can talk about something that is more useful to this class.*

"Quiet!" shouts Mr Harrison. The students stop talking. "Put those comics away! Today I am going to teach you how to grow vegetables. Sometime in the future maybe there will be a time when you have no job. I hope this doesn't happen to you, but it happens to some people. If you are unlucky and have no job, you will have little money. But if you can grow vegetables, you will always have something to eat."

Jimmy hears Mr Harrison. He sits up.

Mr Harrison talks about seeds and plants. He talks about light and water. He talks about how plants need food.

He looks at the class. The students are not interested.

Oh no, thinks Mr Harrison. This was not a good idea.

Then he sees Jimmy Luther. Jimmy is sitting up. He is writing down notes from the blackboard. Mr Harrison is surprised. "Any questions?" asks Mr Harrison.

Jimmy puts up his hand. "Mr Harrison?"

"Yes?"

"Can you tell us about growing tomatoes?"

"Of course," answers Mr Harrison. "What do you want to know?"

"Can I buy seeds for tomatoes? How long does it take for a tomato to grow? How many tomatoes can you get from one plant?"

Mr Harrison is very surprised. *Why is Jimmy interested in tomatoes?* he thinks. This is the first time for Jimmy to ask a question in class. Mr Harrison tries to answer all Jimmy's questions.

Then Jimmy asks, "How much are tomato seeds?"

"About two dollars," says Mr Harrison. "But Jimmy, if you want tomatoes this year you have to buy plants. The plants must go into the ground soon. I planted my tomato seeds about six weeks ago."

"How much are tomato plants?" asks Jimmy.

"Maybe about ten dollars for four plants," says Mr Harrison. "But you need ten or twelve tomato plants."

Jimmy looks sad. He puts his head down on the desk and closes his eyes.

Oh no! thinks Mr Harrison. *Maybe Jimmy wants to grow tomatoes, but he has no money to buy plants. What do I know about him?* Mr Harrison remembers that Jimmy has no father. He thinks Jimmy has a brother or a sister who is younger.

His mother works at night. She has a job cleaning in some big office building. I am sure the family does not have a lot of money. Maybe I can help, he thinks.

The bell rings at the end of the class. The students get up and walk out of the classroom. When Jimmy walks past Mr Harrison's desk, Mr Harrison says, "Jimmy, wait a minute please."

Jimmy and Mr Harrison wait for all the students to go out of the room. Then Mr Harrison says, "I planted many tomato seeds. I was lucky. I got many tomato plants. Would you like some of my plants?"

Jimmy smiles. "Yes please!"

"Come to my office tomorrow after school. I will give you some plants."

"Thank you, Mr Harrison," says Jimmy.

5. JIMMY LUTHER THE GARDENER

The next day, Jimmy goes to Mr Harrison's office. Mr Harrison asks Jimmy, "Why do you want to grow tomatoes?"

Jimmy tells Mr Harrison about the vegetarian restaurant. He tells Mr Harrison about the tomato salad. "I want to try to make some different food. I want to make tomato salad for my mother. I asked my mother to buy tomatoes," he says. "But she says they are too expensive."

"I understand," says Mr Harrison. He teaches Jimmy how to plant the tomatoes. He says, "You have to give the plants water every day." He gives Jimmy a supermarket bag. Inside is some wet newspaper.

"There are twelve plants in there," says Mr Harrison. "Good luck!"

Jimmy says "thank you". He rides his bicycle home. His mother is sleeping. His little sister is playing at her friend's house. Jimmy goes out the back of their house into the garden. The garden is very dirty. There are many weeds and the grass is long. At the end of the garden, there is a small shed. Jimmy tries to open the door. It is difficult to open the door. Jimmy pulls very hard. Suddenly, the door falls down. Jimmy moves back. The door is on the ground.

Oh, no! I have to fix the door, thinks Jimmy. I will fix it later. I want to plant my tomatoes.

The shed is dark, but Jimmy can see some old garden tools in the corner. He takes a spade. He puts the bag with the tomatoes on the floor of the shed.

I'll plant the tomatoes next to the shed, thinks Jimmy. *My mother won't see them there. They will get a lot of sun. It's a good place.*

Jimmy starts to dig. It is very hard work. The ground is very hard. Jimmy is sweating. After thirty minutes he is tired. He looks at the ground.

Maybe that's OK, he thinks. *I can make holes for the tomato plants now.*

He goes back to the shed. He looks for a tool to make holes for the plants. He can't find one. He sees a broken chair.

I can use the leg of the chair to make holes, he thinks.

He breaks a leg of the chair and picks up the bag of plants.

He goes outside. He makes twelve holes.

"You can't do it like that!"

Jimmy is surprised. He looks up. An old man is looking over the wall. It is Mr Lynch. He is the old man who lives next door. Jimmy doesn't like him.

"You can't do it like that!" Mr Lynch says again. "Those holes are too close together. They are not deep enough. They are too close to the wall of the shed."

Jimmy looks down. He doesn't answer. He wants Mr Lynch to go away.

He looks at the holes. Mr Lynch is right. They are too close together. Jimmy worked hard to dig up the ground and make the garden, but it is too small. Jimmy is angry.

Go away, you stupid old man, he thinks. *Leave me alone!*

Bang! Something comes through the air. It almost hits Jimmy on the head. It lands on the ground next to him. It is a trowel. A trowel is a gardening tool to make holes. Mr Lynch threw the trowel over the wall. Jimmy doesn't look at it.

I have twelve plants, he thinks. *Maybe I only need six. Maybe six is enough.*

He makes six new holes using the chair leg. He takes the tomato plants out of the wet newspaper and puts six in the ground. He pushes the earth around the plants. *It is very dry,* he thinks. *I must get water or the plants will die.*

He wraps up the other six plants and puts them in the shed.

Water, thinks Jimmy. *I must get water.* He looks in the shed. There is no bucket. There is no hose. There is no watering can.

Jimmy goes into the house. He looks for something to carry water. He takes a pot from the kitchen. It is not very big, but it is the biggest pot in the kitchen. He goes outside. There is a tap next to the back door of the house. He fills the pot with water and walks down the garden. He pours the water on the ground around the tomatoes. The water disappears. The ground is very dry. Jimmy walks up and down the garden many times. He takes twenty pots of water down to the plants. He is getting tired and bored. He hears a strange sound. *It sounds like a steam train,* he thinks. But he understands. Mr Lynch is watching him and he is laughing.

6. JIMMY LUTHER HAS A VERY BAD DAY

Jimmy is tired. He sleeps well. He doesn't hear his mother come home from work.

The next day is Friday. Jimmy has no time to go outside and look at his tomato plants because his little sister, Joanna, is very unhappy. She had a fight with her best friend. She doesn't want to go to school.

Jimmy tries hard, but it is very difficult. Joanna cries and cries. "I don't want to go to school!"

"Joanna, please be quiet. You will wake Mum."

"I want Mum," says Joanna.

"She's sleeping. Please don't go to her room."

Joanna is noisy, but their mother does not wake up. She does not come into the kitchen. Jimmy is surprised.

He makes peanut butter sandwiches for Joanna. He cuts them into star shapes. He finds some cookies in the back of a cupboard. He puts two cookies into Joanna's lunchbox.

"That's one cookie for you and one for your friend," says Jimmy.

He puts Joanna's lunch box in her backpack and holds her hand. "I'll walk with you to school," he says.

When Jimmy arrives at his school, he is late and he is in trouble. It is not a good start to the day.

In math class, Jimmy opens his book and closes his eyes. *I want a different life,* he thinks. *I want to work at the restaurant in the school holidays. I don't want my mother to work so hard. I want some money. I want a real garden.*

"Jimmy Luther!" The math teacher is talking loudly. Jimmy opens his eyes.

The math teacher is standing next to his desk. The school secretary is standing at the door.

"Please go with Mrs Peters. She has something to tell you. Take your school bag."

Jimmy stands up. He puts his math book in his backpack and goes out of the classroom.

Mrs Peters takes Jimmy to her office. "We got a phone call from the hospital," she says. "Your mother fell over at work last night. She broke her leg. She is in the hospital."

"Last night!" Jimmy is shocked. "She didn't come home! But no one called us. Why didn't we know?"

"I don't know." The school secretary is sad. "But maybe your mother's company doesn't know about you. She had an operation on her leg early this morning. When she woke up, she was very worried about you and your sister. You can go to see her now. Please tell me if I can help you."

Jimmy is walking out the door. "Thank you, Mrs Peters," he says. "But we will be OK."

Jimmy goes to the hospital quickly. His mother is sleeping. He sits next to her bed and holds her hand. His mother wakes up.

"Oh, Jimmy!" she says. "Are you OK? Is Joanna OK?"

"Yes, Mum," says Jimmy. "We are fine."

"But Jimmy!" says his mother. "The doctor says I have to stay in hospital for three weeks! What will you do?"

"We will be fine," says Jimmy.

"But if I don't work, you will have no money!"

"Go to sleep," says Jimmy. "I will bring Joanna to see you tomorrow. Everything is OK. Don't worry."

Jimmy's mother smiles. "You are a good boy," she says and falls asleep.

Jimmy leaves the hospital. *I need a plan,* he thinks. *What can I do? My mother gets money from the company on Friday nights. I need money to buy food,* he thinks. He goes to the office of the cleaning company. "Please give me my mother's money for this week," he says.

They laugh at him. "No," says the manager. "You are a young boy. We will not give your mother's money to you."

Jimmy looks at the clock in the manager's office. *I have to go to Joanna's school. I have to take her home.*

Jimmy goes to Joanna's school quickly. He takes her home.

He says, "Mum had an accident. I will take you to see her tomorrow."

There is only a little food in the house, but Jimmy finds some frozen hamburgers and makes dinner. Joanna is very sad, but Jimmy turns on the TV and says, "You can watch TV tonight. Tomorrow we will go to the hospital."

There is a knock at the door. Jimmy goes to the door. A woman in a suit is standing at the door. One the road outside the house, Jimmy sees a car.

"I am Sally Gibson. I am from the social department for the city. I am here to take your sister to the children's care home."

7. JIMMY LUTHER THE LIAR

Sally Gibson goes into the house. Joanna is sitting on the floor, watching Cartoon Network on the TV.

"Come with me," she says to Joanna. "We will put some clothes in a bag for you."

She says to Jimmy. "Pack some clothes. You will go to the care home for teenage boys."

Joanna starts crying. "I want to stay here! I want my mother!"

"You can't do this!" says Jimmy loudly.

Sally Gibson looks at Jimmy. "Yes, I can. You are too young to stay here alone. You are too young to take care of your sister."

"No!" says Jimmy loudly.

"No," screams Joanna.

Sally Gibson tries to pick Joanna up. Joanna kicks her. Sally Gibson pulls Joanna across the floor. "I'm sorry, Joanna, but you have to come with me. Maybe you can see your brother sometime next week."

"What's all this noise?" Mr Lynch comes into the house.

Joanna runs to Mr Lynch and holds his leg. She is still screaming.

Jimmy is talking loudly.

"Quiet!" says Mr Lynch very loudly.

Joanna stops screaming.

Jimmy stops talking.

"Why are you here?" Mr Lynch asks Sally Gibson.

"I am a social worker. The children's mother is in hospital. She will be there for three weeks. The children cannot stay here alone. I have come to take Joanna to the children's care home and Jimmy to the home for teenage boys."

"They can stay here," says Mr Lynch.

"No, they can't," says Sally Gibson. "There is no one to take care of them."

"Yes, there is," says Mr Lynch. "Me!"

"Who are you?"

"I am Tom Lynch. I live next door."

"I can't leave the children with you. You are not a member of the family."

"I am Mrs Luther's uncle. I live next door. This is my house too. I rent it to my niece very cheaply."

Sally Gibson looks at Jimmy. "Is this true?"

Jimmy looks at Mr Lynch. Sally Gibson cannot see Mr Lynch's face. Mr Lynch looks at Jimmy.

"Yes," says Jimmy. "I don't know about the rent, but he is our mother's uncle."

Sally Gibson does not believe Mr Lynch. She does not believe Jimmy. But it is Friday night. She is tired and she wants to go home.

"OK," she says. "I will come back here on Monday to check that everything is OK."

She walks out of the house.

"Is it true?" Jimmy is very surprised.

Mr Lynch laughs. "I own this house. But no, I am not your mother's uncle. But you can call me Uncle Tom."

"Why did you help us?"

"I don't like screaming and loud voices," says Mr Lynch. "I like peace and quiet."

I don't believe him, thinks Jimmy. *I think he is a very kind man.*

"I will have to stay here with you," says Mr Lynch. "I will sleep in your bed, Jimmy. You can sleep on the sofa."

8. JIMMY LUTHER IS HAPPY

Jimmy does not sleep well. The sofa is old, and it is not comfortable.

Very early on Saturday morning, Jimmy gets up. He remembers his tomato plants. He goes out to look at them.

He is surprised. Next to the shed is a real garden! It has tomato plants and lettuce plants and some new plants. It looks wonderful.

Mr Lynch did this yesterday, he thinks. *I have a real garden.*

He sits on the ground and looks at his garden for a long time.

When Jimmy goes back into the house, Mr Lynch is on the telephone. He is talking loudly.

After a while Mr Lynch puts the phone down. He looks very happy.

"I found your mother's company," he said. "I called them. Your mother had an accident at work. The company has to pay her a lot of money. When she comes back from the hospital, she can stay home for three months. She will not have to work."

Yesterday, I wished for a garden, thinks Jimmy. *Now I have a garden. My mother will not have to work so hard and I can work at the restaurant in the school holidays.*

"Thank you, Uncle Tom," says Jimmy.

THANK YOU

Thank you for reading Jimmy Luther. We hope you enjoyed Jimmy's story. (Word count: 4,724)

There are quizzes about this book on our free study site I Talk You Talk Press EXTRA. http://italk-youtalk.com

If you would like to read more graded readers, please visit our website http://www.italkyoutalk.com

Other Level 1 graded readers include
A Business Trip to New York
A Homestay in Auckland
A Trip to London
Dear Ellen
Emily's Bag
Haruna's Story Part 1
Haruna's Story Part 2
Haruna's Story Part 3
Ken's Story Part 1
Ken's Story Part 2
Life is Surprising!
Strange Stories
The Christmas Present
The Old Hospital
Wei's Part Time Job

We Met Online

We Met Online

ABOUT THE AUTHOR

I Talk You Talk Press is an award-winning Japan-based publisher of language textbooks, graded readers and language learning/teaching resources.

Our team is made up of highly experienced language teachers and translators, who have all studied at least one additional language to an advanced level.

This experience enables us to design our materials from the perspective of both the teacher and the learner. We consult with both teachers and language learners when designing our textbooks and graded readers, and test our materials extensively in the classroom before publication.

We are a fast-growing press, and currently publish graded readers for learners of English. We publish new graded readers monthly.

www.ingramcontent.com/pod-product-compliance
Lightning Source LLC
LaVergne TN
LVHW051517170726
843492LV00002B/987